PASS IT ON

Terra Tarango

Rigby

A Harcourt Achieve Imprint

www.Rigby.com
1-800-531-5015

Carla and her friends were playing at the river. Carla saw some people picking up garbage on the shore. The people were wearing gloves and carrying trash bags.

Carla was curious about the group, so she went over to ask what they were doing. One of the workers, Jenny, said they were helping to keep the river clean.

"Why are you cleaning the river?" Carla asked Jenny.

"Some people who come to the river throw their trash into it," Jenny said. "That makes the water very dirty."

Trash thrown into the water hurts the environment.

"How does all the trash affect the river?" Carla asked.

"Well," Jenny replied, "when trash builds up, some plants and animals can't live in the water anymore."

Carla thought the clean-up team was a good idea. "How does your group work?"

"We get together every May to clean a new river," said Jenny. "We fill lots of trash bags each year."

Volunteers clean thousands of miles of rivers each year.

Carla smiled. "It's a good thing there are people like you who care about the river."

"I enjoy being a part of the clean-up team," Jenny said. "It feels good to help out!"

When rivers are clean, everyone can enjoy them.

feed the hungry?

recycle?

animal rescue?

Carla thought about what Jenny said. Carla decided that she, too, wanted to help out. What would she do?

Carla loved to cook food, so she decided to volunteer at a nearby soup kitchen.

How Do Soup Kitchens Help?

Many people do not have enough food to eat. Soup kitchens and shelters give people food so they do not go hungry.

Soup kitchens depend on volunteers. They need many people to help buy the ingredients, cook the food, and serve it.

Soup Kitchens

It takes a lot of work to feed hungry people. Soup kitchens need as many helpers as possible.

People can also help by donating money or food to a soup kitchen.

While Carla was helping at the soup kitchen, she met a man named Dennis. He thanked her for volunteering. That made Carla feel good.

build homes?

read to children?

plant trees?

Dennis was glad for the help that Carla gave him. He decided that he, too, wanted to help out. What would he do?

Dennis liked to build things, so he decided to help as a homebuilder.

How Do Volunteer Homebuilders Help?

Volunteer homebuilders help build homes for people who need them.

People work together to make sure the houses are built well.

Volunteer Homebuilders

Volunteers work on every part of the house, from the wood frame to the painted walls.

When the house is done, a family in need will have their own home.

While Dennis was working on the house, he met the Smiths, the family who would live in the house. They thanked Dennis for volunteering. That made Dennis feel special.

recycle?

park
clean-up?

Plant trees?

The Smiths were thankful for the work
that Dennis did. They, too, wanted
to help out. What would they do?

The Smiths liked to take care of
their community, so they decided to
recycle old cans and bottles.

How Does Recycling Help?

Many people recycle their aluminum drink cans. About 106,000 cans are recycled every minute!

Recycling is important to our planet. Recycling cuts down on trash and wasted materials.

Recycling

There are many kinds of materials that can be recycled. Many items we use are made from recycled materials.

Recycling and using our resources wisely help to keep our planet clean.

While the Smiths were collecting cans, they met a woman named Eman. She thanked the Smiths for recycling in her neighborhood. That made them feel helpful.

read to children?

crossing guard?

STOP

animal rescue?

Eman was thankful for what the Smiths did. She, too, wanted to help out. What would she do?

Eman liked working with children, so she decided to volunteer at a local school.

How Do School Volunteers Help?

Schools need parents and other volunteers to help students with homework and studying.

Volunteers also help out in other ways. They can help in the library, in the cafeteria, or on field trips.

The next day, Eman went to the school and asked how she could help. The principal thanked her and asked her to read to Ms. García's class.

And guess who's in Ms. García's class—Carla! As Eman left the classroom, Carla said, "Thanks."

Eman said, "You're welcome. JUST PASS IT ON."

These are some ways to volunteer.

VOLUNTEER ACTIVITY	HOW IT HELPS
Park cleanup	Keeps natural areas beautiful and clean
Canned food drive	gets food to people who need it
Tutoring	gives people help learning new things
Fundraising	makes money for a good cause, like protecting animals
Neighborhood watch	helps police protect the community

How can you volunteer?